junie b. jones®

and Some Sneaky Peeky Spying

by BARBARA PARK

illustrated by
Denise Brunkus

Long tail Books

To my editor, Linda Hayward—
Junie B.'s bestest real-life friend

Junie B. Jones and Some Sneaky Peeky Spying by Barbara Park

This bilingual edition was published by Longtail Books in 2021 by arrangement with Barbara Park c/o Writers House LLC through KCC(Korea Copyright Center Inc.), Seoul.

ISBN 979-11-91343-11-3 14740

Longtail, Inc.

Contents

1. Sneaky Peeky Spying 5

2. Questions 17

3. Secret Mystery Guy 27

4. Cookie Mix and Other Stuff 34

5. Sickish 44

6. Squeezy Lips 53

7. Sour Grapes 63

8. Grandparents' Day 73

ABC
Don't
be a
Litter

1
Sneaky Peeky[1] Spying

My name is Junie B. Jones. The B **stands for** Beatrice. **Except** I don't like Beatrice. I just like B and **that's all**.

I go to **kindergarten**. Kindergarten is what comes before first **grade**. Except for I don't know why it's called that **silly** word

1 **peeky** Junie B.가 만들어 낸 말로 단어 'peek(재빨리 훔쳐보다)'의 뒤에 '-y'를 붙여 '훔쳐보는'이라는 의미의 형용사로 사용하였다. 이 책에 나오는 'squeezy' 또한 이와 같은 경우이다.

of kindergarten. 'Cause it should be called zero grade, I think.

My teacher has the name of Mrs.

She has another name, too. But I just like Mrs. and that's all.

Mrs. has short brown hair. And long skirts of wool.[2] And she smiles a real lot.

Except for sometimes when I'm noisy, she **clap**s her loud hands at me.

It used to **scare** me very much. Only then I got used to it. And now I don't even pay it any **attention**.

I wish Mrs. lived next door to me.

Then me and her would be **neighbor**s.

And bestest[3] friends.

---

2 **wool** 울. 양털로 짠 옷감으로 곱슬하며 보온성과 흡습성이 강하다.

And also I could spy on her.

Spying is when you be very quiet. And you look at people through a peeky hole or a **crack** or something.

I am a very good spier.

That's because I have sneaky feet. And my nose doesn't **whistle** when I **breathe**.

Last Friday morning at Grampa[4] Miller house, I hided[5] in the dirty clothes **hamper**.

Then my grampa came in the bathroom. And I **lift**ed up the **lid** a **teeny** bit. And I

---

3 **bestest** 단어 'best(최고의)'를 강조한 비격식적인 표현. '최고로 좋은'이라는 뜻을 나타내며 어린아이가 주로 사용한다.

4 **grampa** '할아버지(grandpa)'를 부르는 말로, 'gramp', 'grampa', 'grampy' 등 다양한 표현이 있다.

5 **hided** (hid) 영어권 국가의 아이들이 동사의 과거형을 말할 때 모든 단어의 끝에 '-ed'를 붙이는 실수를 종종 한다. 이 책에 나오는 'runned(ran)', 'blowed(blew)' 등이 이와 같은 경우이다.

peeked my eyes at him.

And guess what?

Grampa Miller took his whole teeth right out of his head! That's what!

I **pop**ped right out of the hamper!

"HEY! GRAMPA! HOW DID YOU DO THAT CRAZY THING!" I **holler**ed.

Then my grampa **scream**ed very loud. And he runned out of the bathroom **speedy** quick.

Grampa Miller has high blood **pressure**, I think.

Pretty soon Mother hurried into the bathroom with angry feet.

"**That's it**!" she **yell**ed. "No more spying! This is the last time I'm telling you! Do you hear me, missy?[6] Do you?"

"Yes," I said. "'Cause you're hollering right in my ear, that's why."

Then Mother took me home. Except for she kept on staying mad at me.

"Find something quiet to do," she said

---

6 **missy** '아가씨'라는 뜻으로 화나 애정을 담아 어린 여성을 부르는 표현.

kind of **growly**. "Your baby brother has to take his morning **nap**."

So then I thought and thought about what to do. And a very great idea popped into my head.

First, I **took off** my loud shoes . . .

Then I **tip**py-**toe**d into baby Ollie's room in just my sock feet . . .

And I spied on him through the **bar**s in his **crib**.

'Cause what could be quieter than sneaky peeky spying, of course!

Only too bad for me. Because that boring old baby just kept on sleeping and sleeping.

And he wasn't being fun.

So that's how come I **accidental**ly **blow**ed on his face.

And I **tickle**d his nose with a ribbon.

And I shouted, "WAKE UP!" in his ear.

And guess what? Ollie opened his eyes, that's what!

Then he started crying very loud. And Mother runned into his room.

Only she didn't even see me!

'Cause I quick hided in the **closet**!

I smiled to just myself. I'm the bestest spier in the whole wide world, I said inside my head.

That's how come—when I **rode** the bus to school that day—I did a little bit of **brag**ging.

"I'm the bestest spier in the whole world," I said to my bestest friend named Grace.

Then I took off my shoes. And I showed

her my sneaky sock feet.

"See?" I said. "See how quiet they are? You can **hardly** even hear those guys."

After that, I breathed in and out for her.

"And see? My nose doesn't whistle, either," I said.

That Grace smiled. "I'm good at spying, too," she said.

I **pat**ted her. "Yeah, only too bad, Grace. But you can't be as good as me. 'Cause I said it first."

That Grace did a mad breath at me. It is called a **huffy**,[7] I think.

"I heard your nose whistle, Grace," I told her.

---

7 **huffy** 주니 B.가 명사형 'huff(씩씩거림)'가 생각나지 않아 형용사형 'huffy(성내는)'로 잘못 말한 것이다.

Just then the bus got to school. And me and that Grace **race**d each other to the **playground**.

Except for she **beat**ed me. Only it didn't **count**. 'Cause I wasn't really racing.

Then we played horses with my other bestest friend named Lucille. Only pretty soon the bell rang. And we all runned to Room Nine speedy quick.

Mrs. was at the door waiting for us.

"Good afternoon, ladies," she said.

"Good afternoon, lady," I said back very **polite**.

Then Mrs. smiled at me.

That's because she is the nicest teacher I ever saw.

And so I wish me and her were bestest

friends.

And guess what else?

I wish I could hide in her hamper.

2
Questions

Me and my bestest friend Lucille sit at my same table together.

My table is where I sit up straight.

And do my work.

And don't talk to my **neighbor**.

Except I keep on forgetting that part.

"I wonder where Mrs. lives?" I **whisper**ed to Lucille real quiet.

"Shh," said Lucille. "We can't talk or else

we'll get in trouble. And anyway, you're not allowed to know where she lives. 'Cause it's a secret."

"Says who?" I asked.

"Says my brother, that's who. And he's in third **grade**. And he says teachers have to keep their house a secret. Or else kids might go there and throw **rotten** tomatoes."

I did a **huffy** at her.

"Yeah, only I don't want to throw rotten tomatoes, Lucille," I explained. "I just want to hide in her **hamper**, and **that's all**."

"I don't care," she said. "You're still not allowed. 'Cause my brother said so. And he knows more than you do. So there."

I made an angry face. *"So there* is not a

nice word, Lucille," I said.

Then I made a **fist** at her. Except for Mrs. saw me. And so I had to un**fold** it.

After that I behaved myself very good. I sat up real straight. And I did all my work.

Work is when you use your brain and a pencil.

Only sometimes I **accidental**ly use the eraser too hard. And a big hole **rub**s in my paper.

"Hey! I did beautifully today!" I called out. "'Cause guess what? No hole! That's what!"

Mrs. came to my table. She put a gold star on my work.

"You *did* do beautifully, Junie B.," she said. "Maybe I'll hang this one on the wall for Grandparents' Day on Monday. Would you like that?"

"Yes," I said. "Only I keep on forgetting how come those guys are coming to this place."

Then Mrs. explained to me all about Grandparents' Day again.

She said our grandparents are coming for a visit. And we get to show them Room Nine. And also we get to have **'freshment**s together.

Mrs. said 'freshments are cookies and a**beverage**.

I raised my hand.

"Yeah, only I don't think I'm allowed to have the kind of drink named abeverage. 'Cause I'm only allowed to have milk and juice and that's all."

Mrs. looked up at the **ceiling** with her eyes. Then I looked up there, too. But I didn't see anything.

"How many of you think you can bring cookies on Monday?" asked Mrs.

"I CAN! I CAN!" I **holler**ed very excited. "'CAUSE MY MOTHER IS THE BESTEST COOKIE BAKER IN THE WHOLE WORLD, THAT'S WHY! EXCEPT FOR ONE TIME SHE ACCIDENTALLY FORGOT THEY WERE IN THE OVEN. AND THE FIREMEN HAD TO COME TO OUR HOUSE."

Mrs. laughed. Only I don't know why. 'Cause that was not a funny story.

After that, she gave me a note for

Mother. It was some writing about baking cookies, I think.

"If your mother has any questions, please tell her to call me," said Mrs.

Just then I got a very great idea!

"Hey!" I said. "Maybe me and Mother can bring the cookies to your house! And

so then I can see where you live!"

Mrs. **rumple**d my hair. "You don't have to come to my house, Junie B. Just bring the cookies to school on Monday morning."

I smiled very sweet. "Yeah, only I still want to see where you live," I said.

Then Mrs. turned around. And she

walked back to her desk.

That's how come I had to follow her.

"Do you have the rich kind of house? Or the **regular** kind of house?" I asked her. "'Cause I just have the regular kind of house. Except for Mother wants the rich kind. Only Daddy said *lotsa luck*.[1]"

Mrs. pointed at my chair. That means to sit down, I think.

"Yeah, only do you have a daddy that lives at your house, too? Are there any pictures of him in your wallet? Let's look in there, okay? Do you have a secret **compartment** in it? 'Cause my grampa Miller has one of those things with fifty

1 **lotsa luck** 'lots of luck(행운을 빈다)'을 축약한 비격식적인 표현.

bucks[2] in it. Only don't tell Grandma."

Mrs. took my hand. Then me and her walked back to my table.

"Yeah, only guess what I'm wondering now? Now I'm wondering what your bedtime is. 'Cause my bedtime is when the little hand is at the seven, and the big hand is at the six. Only I hate that **dumb** stupid bedtime. 'Cause I'm not even tired yet, of course."

Mrs. put her finger up to her **lip**s.

"That's enough, Junie B.," she said. "I **mean** it. I want you to **settle** down now."

Then she went right back to the front of the room. And she didn't answer any of

---

2 **buck** 미국이나 호주, 뉴질랜드의 달러를 이르는 비격식적인 표현.

my questions.

'Cause guess why?

Mrs. is a secret **mystery** guy. That's why.

3
Secret Mystery Guy

Me and my bestest friend Grace **rode** the bus home together.

That's when I told her about Mrs. and her secret house.

"Mrs. is a secret mystery guy," I said. "'Cause she wouldn't answer any of my questions. And so now I have **curiosity** about her."

That Grace **wrinkle**d her **eyebrow**s.

"Me, too," she said. "Now I have curiosity about her, too."

I **pat**ted her again. "Yeah, only too bad, Grace. But you can't have as much as me. 'Cause I said it first, remember that?"

That Grace did another **huff**y at me.

"Whoops. Your nose is still **whistling**, Grace," I said.

A few minutes later, I got off the bus. I runned to my house like a **speedy** rocket.

"GRANDMA! GRANDMA!" I shouted very excited. "IT'S ME! IT'S JUNIE B. JONES! I'M HOME FROM MY SCHOOL!"

Grandma Miller **babysit**s me and baby Ollie when Mother is at work.

She was in the kitchen **feed**ing Ollie **sprain**ed **pea**s.[1]

"GUESS WHAT, GRANDMA! GUESS WHAT? MY TEACHER IS A SECRET MYSTERY GUY! AND SHE WON'T TELL ME WHERE SHE LIVES. ONLY I WANT TO GO TO HER HOUSE VERY BAD!"

Grandma Miller **shush**ed me. "There's no need to shout, Junie B.," she said. "I'm right here."

"Yeah, only I can't help it, Grandma! 'Cause I have curiosity about her!"

Grandma Miller did a little smile. "Curiosity killed the cat,[2] you know," she said.

---

1 **sprained peas** 완두콩을 삶아 으깬 뒤 물을 조금 넣고 걸쭉하게 만드는 이유식인 'strained peas'를 잘못 말한 것이다. 'sprain'은 '삐다, 접지르다'라는 뜻이다.

2 **curiosity killed the cat** 직역하면 '호기심이 고양이를 죽였다'라는 뜻으로, '호기심이 지나치면 위험하다'라는 의미의 숙어이다.

Then my mouth went open. And my eyes got very big too.

"What cat, Grandma? Where did the curiosity kill it? Was it in the street by my school? 'Cause I saw a **squish**ed cat in the street by my school. Only Paulie Allen Puffer said it got **run**ned **over** by the ice cream truck."

Grandma Miller looked at me for a very long time. Then she went to the **sink**. And she took an aspirin.[3]

Just then I heard a noise at the front door.

And its name is Mother was home from work!

"MOTHER! MOTHER! I HAVE A

---

3 **aspirin** 아스피린. 해열, 진통, 항염에 작용하는 가정상비약.

'PORTANT NOTE FROM MRS. 'CAUSE YOU AND ME ARE GOING TO BAKE DELICIOUS COOKIES. AND THEN WE CAN TAKE THEM TO HER HOUSE AND SEE WHERE SHE LIVES!"

Mother read the note.

"The note says to take the cookies to school, Junie B. Not to your teacher's house."

"Yeah, only I already know that. But my teacher is a secret mystery guy. And she won't tell me where she lives. And so you and me have to find it ourselves."

Mother shook her head. "**No way, toots,**[4]" she said.

---

4 **toots** '아가씨'라는 뜻으로 애정을 담아 장난스럽게 어린 여성을 부르는 표현.

"Yes way!" I hollered. "We have to! 'Cause now I've got curiosity in me. And I have to find out where her house is. Or else Grandma said I'm gonna get runned over by an ice cream truck."

Then Mother did a **frown** at Grandma. And Grandma took another aspirin.

"Your teacher is *not* a secret mystery guy, Junie B.," said Mother. "She's just a **regular** person. With a regular family. And there's no way that you and I are going to **bother** her at her house."

I **stamp**ed my foot. "YES WE ARE! WE ARE TOO! 'CAUSE I WANT TO, THAT'S WHY!"

After that, I got sended to my room.

'Cause of no shouting. And no stamping

my foot. Only I never even heard of that **dumb rule** before.

I shut my door very angry. Then I put my head under my **pillow**. And I called Mother the name of pewie head.[5]

"And guess what else?" I said very quiet. "Teachers are not regular people.

"So there. Ha ha."

---

5 **pewie head** 주니 B.가 '바보', '멍청이'라는 의미로 만든 말.

4

Cookie Mix[1] and Other Stuff

The next day was Saturday.

Saturday is the day me and my mother go to the **grocery** store.

I have **rule**s at that place.

Like no **holler**ing the words I WANT ICE CREAM!

And no calling Mother the name of big

1 **cookie mix** 쿠키 믹스. 쿠키를 손쉽게 만들어 먹을 수 있도록 기본 재료들을 혼합하여 놓은 가루.

meanie when she won't buy it.

And no eating a bag of marshmallows[2] that doesn't belong to you.

Or else the store guy **yank**s it away from you. And he says, *Eating is the same thing as* ***steal****ing, young lady.*

Then he takes you to Mother. And she has to pay for the whole **entire** bag. **Except** for I don't know why. 'Cause I only ate three of those softy guys and **that's all**.

The carts at the grocery store have seats in them. That's where babies sit. Only not me. 'Cause big girls get to walk all **by theirselves**.

And guess what else? One time Mother

---

2 **marshmallow** 마시멜로. 젤라틴, 달걀 흰자, 설탕, 향료, 식용 색소 등을 섞어 만든 쫄깃한 과자.

even let me push the whole big cart without any help.

Except for then some baked beanies[3] got **knock**ed off their **shelf**. And a grandma got her foot caught in my tire. And so now I have to wait till I'm bigger.

My favorite **aisle** is where the cookies are. That's 'cause sometimes there is a lady at a table there. And she gives me and Mother cookie **sample**s. And we don't even have to pay for them.

Their name is **freebie**s, I think.

Only too bad for me. 'Cause this time the lady wasn't there.

---

3 **baked beanies** 토마토소스에 넣어 삶은 강낭콩 통조림을 이르는 'baked beans'를 주니 B.가 'baked beanies'라고 장난스럽게 말한 표현.

"Darn it,[4]" I said very **disappoint**ed. "No freebie lady."

Mother smiled. "That's okay. When we get home, we're going to bake our own cookies for Grandparents' Day, remember? Won't that be fun?" she asked.

I made my **shoulder**s go up and down.

That's 'cause I was still mad at her for not taking me to my teacher's house, of course.

"What kind of cookie mix do you want?" asked Mother.

I did a **frown** at her. "I don't even want to bake cookies anymore," I said. "'Cause you still won't take me to where Mrs.

---

4 **darn it** 'damn it(빌어먹을, 제기랄)'을 순화한 단어로, 못마땅하거나 짜증스러울 때 쓰는 속어.

lives."

Mother **rumple**d my hair. "Staying mad isn't going to change things, Junie B.," she said. "Now do you want to pick out the cookie mix? Or shall I?"

Then Mother picked out some cookie mix. And she gave it to me. And I throwed it in the cart very hard.

"Thank you," said Mother.

"You're not welcome," I said.

After that, Mother took me outside of the store. And me and her had a little talk.

A little talk is when Mother is mad at me. And she says who do I think I am, missy? And **zact**ly how long do I think she's going to **put up with** me?

ILK
1/2 gal.
GRA
2 lb.
$1.5

Then I have to say a **'pology** to her.

A 'pology is the words *I'm sorry.*

Except for you don't actually have to **mean** it. 'Cause nobody can even tell the difference.

After the little talk, we went back into the store.

"Shall we try again?" asked Mother.

Then she gave me another box of cookie mix. And I put it in the cart very nice.

"That's better," she said. "Thank you."

You're not welcome, I said inside my head.

Then I smiled to just myself. 'Cause Mother can't even hear me in there.

After that, me and her went around the corner. And I saw my most favorite[5] thing in the whole world!

And its name is the **water fountain**!

"Hey! I need a drink!" I said very excited.

Then I runned right over there. And I **hop**ped up on the little step.

"Need some help?" called Mother.

"No," I said. "'Cause I'm almost six years old, that's why. And so I already know how to work this big guy.

"And here's another thing I know," I said. "No putting your mouth on the water **spout**. Or else **germ**s will get inside you. And you will die."

---

5 **most favorite** '가장 좋아하는'이라는 뜻을 지닌 비격식적인 표현. 원래는 단어 'favorite'이 '선호하는'이라는 의미를 나타내기 때문에 형용사의 최상급을 만드는 부사인 'most'를 잘 붙이지 않는다.

I smiled very **proud**. "Paulie Allen Puffer told me that," I explained.

Then I **bend**ed my head over the fountain. And I drank for a very long time.

"Hurry up, Junie B.," said Mother. "I need to get the shopping done."

I **wipe**d my mouth off with my arm.

"Yeah, only I can't hurry up. Or else I might get a **stomachache** and **spit** up water. 'Cause a boy named William did that on the **playground** yesterday."

Mother looked at her watch. "Okay. Well, I'm going to be right here in the cereal aisle. As soon as you've finished drinking, come directly back to me."

"Okey-dokey,[6]" I said very happy.

Then I turned around and drinked and drinked and drinked.

Except for then I started feeling a little bit **sickish**. And so I had to sit down on the little step and **rest** my water.

That's when the big front doors of the grocery store opened.

And guess what?

My eyes almost **pop**ped out of my head, that's what!

'Cause I saw a big shock!

And its name was Mrs.!

My **real live** teacher named Mrs. was at the grocery store!!!

---

6 **okey-dokey** 긍정의 대답을 나타내는 'Okay', 'OK'의 비격식적인 표현.

5
Sickish

Mrs. didn't see me.

That's because I hided behind the **water fountain speedy** fast.

And guess what?

She had a *man* with her!

And I never even saw that guy before!

"Hey! Who the heck[1] is that?" I said to

---

1 **heck** '도대체', '젠장' 또는 '제기랄'이라는 뜻으로 당혹스럽거나 짜증스러운 감정을 강조하는 속어.

just myself.

Then I runned my fastest to the cereal **aisle**, to tell Mother what I saw.

Only **all of a sudden** I remembered about how she told me *no more* ***spying***. And so maybe I might get in trouble with her, I think.

That's how come I stopped running. And I started to go back to **peek** at Mrs. some more. But Mother already **spot**ted me.

"Hey! Where are you going?" she called at me. "Come here."

"Yeah, only I can't come there," I explained. "'Cause I just remembered something very important. And it's called—I'm not done drinking yet!"

Then I runned right back to the water fountain. Only Mrs. and the strange man were already **disappear**ed.

"Shoot,[2]" I said. "Where did those **Sneaky** Petes[3] go to?"

After that I had to look all over the store for those guys.

First, I looked where the chocolate milk was. Then I looked where the pasketti[4] and tomato sauce was. And I also looked where the delicious candy was.

Only guess where I finally found them?

At the **stinky dumb** vegetables! That's

---

2 **shoot** '이런' 또는 '젠장'이라는 뜻으로 못마땅하거나 짜증스러울 때 쓰는 속어.

3 **Sneaky Petes** '믿을 수 없는 사람', '수상한 행동을 하는 사람'을 뜻하는 속어.

4 **pasketti** 영어권 국가의 어린아이들이 흔히 하는 실수로, 'spaghetti(스파게티)'를 잘못 말한 것이다.

where!

I quick **duck**ed down and hided around the corner.

Then I did some sneaky peeky spying on them.

I saw Mrs. picking out **yucky** blucky[5] brockly.[6]

And stewie pewie tomatoes.[7]

And also the kind of vegetable named Sue Keeny.[8]

Except for then the strange man **snatch**ed Sue Keeny right out of her

---

5 **yucky blucky** '구역질 나는', '역겨운'이라는 뜻의 속어.

6 **brockly** 주니 B.가 채소 'broccoli(브로콜리)'를 잘못 말한 것이다.

7 **stewie pewie tomatoes** 주니 B.가 '역겨운 스튜를 만드는 토마토'라는 의미로 만든 말장난. 스튜 요리를 뜻하는 'stewed'와 역겨움을 나타내는 표현 'pew(P.U.)'를 변형해 'tomatoes' 앞에 붙였다.

8 **sue keeny** 주니 B.가 채소 'zucchini(주키니)'를 잘못 말한 것이다. 주키니는 오이와 비슷한 모양을 한 짙은 녹색의 호박으로, 주로 애호박보다 크고 통통하다.

hands. And he tried to put it back on the **shelf**.

Only Mrs. **grab**bed it right back again. And she **pretend**ed to hit him on the head with it. And then they both started laughing very much.

That's when a very terrible thing happened.

And it's called—Mrs. and the strange man did a big **smooch**ie kiss!

And it was in front of the whole **entire** everybody!

I **cover**ed my eyes. That's 'cause I was **shamed** of her, of course. **On account of** teachers shouldn't do that smoochie thing!

After that, I peeked my eyes between my fingers. And I saw Mrs. standing at the grapes.

She picked up a **bunch** of the green kind. Then she pulled some grapes right off the top of it.

And that's when the most terriblest[9] thing of all happened!

Because just then, Mrs. put the grapes in her mouth!

And she ATE them!

Mrs. ATE the GRAPES!

And she didn't even PAY for them!

"Oh no," I **whisper**ed very **upset**. "Oh no. Oh no."

'Cause eating is the same thing as **steal**ing, remember?

---

9 **most terriblest** 형용사 'terrible'의 최상급을 잘못 만든 것으로, 올바른 표현은 'most terrible'이다.

And teachers **are**n't **supposed to** do stealing! Teachers are supposed to be perfecter[10] than that! 'Cause they have to set a good **zample** for little children!

After that I felt very sickish inside of my

---

10 perfecter 형용사 'perfect'의 비교급을 잘못 만든 것으로, 올바른 표현은 'more perfect'이다.

APPL
GRA

stomach.

On account of Mrs. didn't even get caught and learn her **lesson**!

'Cause nobody saw what she did!

Not the store guy.

Not the strange man.

Nobody.

Nobody except for me.

6
Squeezy Lips

I didn't **tattletale**[1] on Mrs.

That's 'cause if I told Mother, I would get in trouble for spying.

And if I told the store guy, Mrs. might go to **jail**.

And so I just keeped it a secret inside my head.

---

1 **tattletale** 주로 명사 또는 형용사로 쓰이는 단어 'tattletale(고자질쟁이, 고자질하는)'을 여기에서는 '고자질하다'라는 의미의 동사처럼 사용했다.

'Cause nobody can see secrets inside your head.

Not even if they look in your ears.

On Sunday Grandma and Grampa Miller came to our house for dinner. Only I couldn't talk to them that much.

That's because secrets are very **slippery**. And I didn't want it to **slip** out of my mouth by **accident**.

"Why so quiet tonight, Junie B.?" said Grandma Miller at the table. "Cat got your **tongue**?[2]"

My mouth went wide open.

---

2 **(has the) cat got your tongue?** 직역하면 '고양이가 혀를 물어갔나요?'라는 뜻으로, '왜 이렇게 말이 없나요?' 혹은 '왜 아무 말도 없나요?' 라고 물어볼 때 사용하는 숙어이다.

"What cat, Grandma? Is it the same cat that got killed by the ice cream truck? How come he wants to get my tongue? Did his tongue get **squish**ed in the accident?"

Grandma Miller **made a face**. Then she didn't eat her roast beef[3] anymore.

Mother looked surprised at me. "You sure did get **chatty all of a sudden**. Does this mean you're not mad about the cookies anymore?"

And so then I remembered to stop talking again. Or else my secret might slip out.

I squeezed my lips together very tight.

---

3 **roast beef** 로스트비프. 큰 덩어리째로 오븐에 구운 쇠고기 요리.

And guess what else? Even the next day—when I was on the bus to school—my lips still stayed squeezed.

"Hi, Junie B.," said my bestest friend Grace.

I did a **wave** at her.

That Grace **frown**ed at me. "How come you're not saying hi? You *have* to say hi. It's the **rule**s."

Except for I still didn't say hi.

And so then she called me the name of big **stinky**.

And when we got to school, that Grace told Lucille I was being a **meanie**. And so those two played horses all **by theirselves**.

And not me.

That's how come I finally had to sing

something very loud at them.

"I'VE GOT A SECRET! HA-HAHA-HA-HAAAA-HAAA," I sang.

That Grace put her hands on her **hip**s.

"So?" she said. "We don't care. Do we, Lucille?"

Except for just then Lucille runned over to me speedy quick. 'Cause she cared, that's why.

"If you tell me your secret, I'll be your best friend," she said.

"Yeah, only I can't, Lucille," I explained. "'Cause if I tell you my secret, Mrs. might get in big trouble. And so I have to keep it inside my head."

Lucille did a frown at me.

"It's not good to keep secrets inside your

head, Junie B.," she said. "My brother says keeping secrets inside your head makes **pressure** in there. And pretty soon your head **blow**s up."

My eyes got very big at her.

"Oh no!" I **holler**ed real **upset**.

Then I holded my head real tight with my hands. And I runned my very fastest to the nurse's office.[4] 'Cause she has Band-Aids[5] to hold your head together, I think.

"MY HEAD'S GONNA BLOW! MY HEAD'S GONNA BLOW!" I **yell**ed at the nurse.

She jumped up from her desk and

---

4 **nurse's office** 보건실. 학교나 회사에서, 학생이나 사원의 건강이나 위생 등을 위해 적절한 보호 및 관리를 할 수 있는 시설.

5 **Band-Aid** 반창고. 'Band-Aid'는 본래 미국 회사에서 사용하는 상표명이었으나, 반창고를 일컫는 일반적인 용어로 굳어졌다.

hurried over to me.

"What's wrong, Junie B.? Do you have a bad **headache**?" she asked.

"No. I have a bad *secret*. It's about Mrs. Only I can't tell anybody! And now there's pressure in my head. And I need a Band-Aid. Or else it's gonna **splode**!"

The nurse said **calm** down to me. Then she put a Band-Aid on my head. And me and her went to **Principal**'s office.

Principal is the boss of the school.

Me and him know each other very good.

That's because I keep on getting sent down there. And so now I'm not even afraid of that guy.

Principal sat me in a big wood chair.

"Good afternoon, Junie B.," he said. "What's the trouble today?"

"Good afternoon," I said back. "My head's gonna blow."

Principal frowned his eyes at me. "Why do you think that?" he asked.

I did a little bit of **squirm**ing. "'Cause I got a secret in there, that's why," I said.

Principal sat down at his big desk. He **fold**ed his hands.

"Maybe if you tell me your secret, I can help you," he said.

"Yeah, only I can't talk," I told him.

Principal looked **disappoint**ed at me. "But I thought you and I were **pal**s," he said.

"We are," I said. "I'm not even afraid of you."

Principal did a **chuckle**. "Good. That's good," he said. "Then why don't you tell me what's **bother**ing you."

That's when I did a **huffy** breath at him.

'Cause the guy wasn't listening to me, of course.

"Yeah, only I already said I can't talk, remember that? 'Cause if I talk, then I might **accidental**ly tell you that my teacher stoled[6] grapes at the **grocery** store. And then she might have to go to jail. And so that's how come I just have to keep it a secret inside my head. And **that's all**."

I **smooth**ed my skirt. "The end," I said.

Then I squeezed my lips together very tight. Or else my secret might slip out.

Only guess what?

I think it already did.

---

6 **stoled** (stole) 여기에서는 주니 B.가 동사 'steal'의 불규칙 과거형인 'stole'의 끝에 다시 '-ed'를 붙이는 실수를 한다. 이 책에 나오는 'tooked(took)' 또한 이와 같은 경우이다.

7
Sour Grapes

Principal called Mrs. to come to his office.

Only I didn't even know he was going to do that **sneaky** thing.

That's how come I had to pull my skirt way over my head. Or else Mrs. would see me there. And she would know I **tattletale**d on her.

"Don't do that," said Principal.

"Yeah, only I'm allowed," said from

underneath my skirt. "'Cause I have on my new red tights.[1] And also boxer shorts.[2]"

After that, Principal went out of his

1 **tights** 타이츠, 팬티스타킹. 주로 어린이들이 방한용으로 신는, 허리까지 오는 긴 양말을 말한다.

2 **boxer shorts** 복서 쇼츠. 허리선에 고무줄을 넣어 입는 헐렁하고 짧은 반바지를 말한다.

office. And I heard my teacher's voice outside the door.

Then I quick got down from my big wood chair. And I hided under Principal's **giant** desk. 'Cause I was **scare**d of what was going to happen, that's why.

I stayed quiet for lots of minutes.

Then I heard feet come back in the office. And so I made my breath very quiet.

"Junie? Junie B. Jones?" said Principal.

"She might be hiding," said Mrs. "She's good at that, you know."

And so just then I had to think of something very quick. Or else they might come looking for me, I think.

"Yeah, only Junie B. Jones isn't hiding," said in a **scary** voice. "Junie B. Jones had to go home. Only don't call her mother. Or else she will get mad at you and **crack** your head open."

After that, feet walked real fast around the desk. It was Principal.

"Come out of there right now, young lady," he said.

I **peek**ed my eyes at him.

"Shoot," I said very quiet.

Then I had to sit in the big wood chair again. And Mrs. sat down next to me. Except for I didn't look at her. Or else she might be making a **fist** at me.

"Good afternoon, Junie B.," she said in a nice voice.

I did a **gulp**.

"I think you and I need to have a little talk," she said.

Then my eyes got a **teeny** bit of wet in them. 'Cause a little talk means I'm gonna get **yell**ed at.

"Yeah, only I tried not to tattletale on

you," I said very quick. "'Cause I didn't want you to go to **jail** for **steal**ing grapes. And so I kept it a secret inside my head. And I didn't talk. And Grandma Miller thought a dead cat got my **tongue**.

"Only today Lucille said my head was gonna blow. And so that's how come I runned to the nurse for a Band-Aid. And she tooked me to Principal. And then my secret accidentally **slip**ped out of my **lip**s."

Mrs. dried my eyes with a **tissue**.

"It's okay, Junie B.," she said. "I'm not angry at you. I just need to know what you saw me do at the grocery store. Can you tell me what you saw?"

Then she said the word ***egg-zactly***.

I made my voice very **whisper**ing. "I

egg-zactly saw you eat grapes," I told her. "Except for you didn't pay the store man for them. You just put them in your mouth and ate them. And that is called the word of stealing, I think."

After that I hided my head under my skirt again.

"You don't have to hide, Junie B.," said Mrs. "*I'm* the one who should be hiding. *I'm* the one who took the grapes."

I peeked my eyes over my skirt at her.

Then Mrs. did a little smile. And she explained all about what happened.

"Two weeks ago I bought some grapes at the grocery store," she said. "But when I got them home I **discover**ed they were so sour no one in my family would eat them.

"So *this* week—when my husband and I went back to the store—I thought I'd be smart and taste a couple of grapes before I bought them."

I raised my **eyebrows**. "Is that the **rules**?" I asked very quiet.

Mrs. shook her head.

"No," she said. "That's *not* the rules. I should have told the grocery man about my sour grapes. And then I should have asked him if I could **sample** one or two. But I didn't do that. And it was right of you to worry when you saw me eating them without paying for them."

"It was?" I asked.

Mrs. smiled again. "Of course it was," she said. "It shows you know right from wrong. And it also shows that teachers make mistakes just like everybody else. Teachers aren't perfect, Junie B. *No* one is perfect."

After that I felt **relief** in me. 'Cause of no more secret, that's why.

"Yeah, and guess what else I saw?" I said very happy. "I saw you and your strange man do a big **smooch**ie kiss. And it was right in front of the whole **entire** everybody! Only you didn't even know I was **spy**ing on you! 'Cause I'm not actually allowed to do that sneaky thing. Only my mother never even finded out!"

I smiled very **proud** of myself.

Except for Mrs. didn't smile back.

And Principal didn't smile back, too.

'Cause guess why?

Another secret just slipped out.

That's why.

8
Grandparents' Day

Mrs. went back to Room Nine. That's because the bell rang to start **kindergarten**, of course.

Only **Principal** didn't let me go too.

He said to stay in my wood chair.

Then he called Mother on the telephone. And he told her all about the **grocery** store. And also about my **sneaky peek**y **spy**ing.

Principal is a **squeal**er.

After that, Mother said she wanted to talk to me. Only when I said hi, she didn't even say hi back.

She said she wasn't very happy with me, missy. And no more spying means no more spying. And we would talk about this after her work.

Then Mother said she never wants to get any more phone calls from Principal. Did I understand? Did I? Did I?

I looked at Principal.

"Mother says not to call her anymore," I told him.

Then Mother did a loud **groan** in the phone. **Except** I don't know why.

After that, me and her **hang**ed **up**. And Principal said I could go to Room Nine.

And so I runned there **speedy** quick.

Only too bad for me. 'Cause I got there too late to sing "My Country Tizzy Thee . . . Sweet Land of Liver Free.[1]" Which is my favorite **flag** song.

And so I just had to sit down at my table, and **that's all**.

I showed Lucille my Band-Aid.

"See? My head's not **blow**ed up," I said very happy.

"Too bad," said a **mean** boy named Jim.

I made a **fist** at him.

Then me and him got into a **scuffle**.

Scuffle is the school word for I

---

1 **My Country Tizzy Thee . . . Sweet Land of Liver Free** 1931년 이전에 사용되었던 미국 국가. 원래 가사는 'My country 'tis of thee, Sweet land of liberty'이지만 주니 B.가 잘못 말하고 있다.

accidentally **tore** his shirt.

Only guess what? I didn't even get in trouble!

'Cause just then the grandparents came to Room Nine for Grandparents' Day!

"HEY! THERE'S MINE! THERE'S MINE!" I **holler**ed very excited. "MINE IS THE GRAMPA WITH THE **BALDIE** HEAD!"

"Mine too!" said a girl named Charlotte.

"Mine too!" said my boyfriend named Ricardo.

Then a grandma with **blond** hair came in. And she had on long red **fingernail**s. And **dangling** earrings with **jewel**s on them.

"That's my **nanna**!" said Lucille.

I smiled at her. "Your nanna looks like a **moneybag**s, Lucille," I said.

After that, another grandma came in. And she runned over to that Jim I hate. And she tried to **hug** him very tight.

Only that mean Jim just kept on standing there. And he didn't even hug her back.

I **tap**ped on her.

"I will hug you," I said.

And so then me and her hugged real tight.

"I hate your grandboy," I said very sweet.

Just then Mrs. **clap**ped her loud hands together. And she made the grandparents

A B C D E F G H I J K L M

sit down in the back of the room.

Then the children talked all about what we do in Room Nine.

"It is fun here," said my bestest friend, that Grace. "We learn to **count**. And to read. And to wash our hands after we go to the bathroom."

"And we learn **recess** and **snack**s and art," said Ricardo.

"Art is my favorite," I called out. "Only my art didn't get hanged up. 'Cause I painted a horse. And his head **turn**ed **out** like a fat wiener sausage.[2] And so I had to tear it up and **stomp** on it with my shoes."

2 **wiener sausage** 비엔나소시지. 손가락같이 가늘고 짧은 소시지. 쇠고기나 돼지고기로 만들며, 오스트리아 빈에서 처음 시작되었다고 한다.

Then that mean Jim did a cuckoo **sign**[3] at me.

And it was right in front of the whole **entire** grandparents!

"Yeah, only everybody makes mistakes!" I said. "Right, Mrs.? Right? 'Cause on Saturday you kissed a strange man at the grocery store. And then you **stole**d a **bunch** of grapes. And so even teachers make mistakes. Right?"

Mrs.'s face went funny. Then her **skin** turned the color of **reddish**. And her voice couldn't say any words.

"How come you're not talking, Mrs.?" I hollered out. "Does the dead cat got your

---

3 **cuckoo sign** '미쳤다'라는 의미로 관자놀이 주변에서 손가락을 빙빙 돌리는 행동을 말한다.

tongue?"

Just then Grandma Miller made a loud laugh in the back of the room.

Then I heard my grampa laugh, too.

And pretty soon, lots of other grandparents were laughing and laughing.

"HEY! IT SOUNDS HAPPY IN THIS PLACE!" I hollered.

After that, Mrs. didn't look so reddish anymore.

Then we got out the **'freshment**s. And Grandma Miller helped me put my cookies on a plate.

Mrs. made a **'nounce**ment to Room Nine. And she said only two cookies **apiece** for the children.

Except for I ate four delicious chocolate

ones. And nobody even saw me!

Only that's not called stealing.

That's called ***extras***.

After the 'freshments, the grandparents had to go home to their houses.

And so I hugged my grandma and grandpa very much.

And then I hugged that mean Jim's grandma too.

And also Lucille's moneybags nanna.

"Love your earrings," I said.

Then Mrs. saw me being **polite**. And she smiled very nice at me.

Mrs. has white teeth.

They are just like Grampa Miller's teeth. Only hers don't come out, I think.

Except I'm not for sure **positive**.

And so guess what?

I still wish I could hide in her **hamper**.

That's what.